HORROR WRITING PROMPTS

77 POWERFUL IDEAS TO INSPIRE YOUR FICTION

by Rayne Hall

HORROR WRITING PROMPTS:
77 POWERFUL IDEAS TO INSPIRE YOUR FICTION

by Rayne Hall

Book cover by Erica Syverson and Uros Jovanovic

© 2017 Rayne Hall

May 2017 Edition

ISBN-13: 978-1545482698

ISBN-10: 1545482691

British English.

INTRODUCTION

This book is crammed with fertile seeds for fiction that will thrill, disturb or scare your readers. Each prompt comes with a wealth of suggestions for how you can develop it to suit the kind of story you want to write. Plant those seeds into the rich ground of your own imagination, and watch them grow.

All you need is a timer (such as a stopwatch, kitchen timer or computer app), and a keyboard or pen. Many writers find that their creativity flows best when they write by hand, but the choice is yours.

Step 1: Set the timer to 10 minutes. Pick a prompt at random, and jot down whatever ideas it suggests. Some prompts have pictures, and you choose whether to write about the complete image or to zoom in on any aspect of the picture that intrigues you. Without evaluating the ideas or censoring your thoughts, just keep the pen moving on the paper or the fingers dancing on the keyboard. This process is called 'freewriting'. Whenever your thoughts dry up, write "What if...?", a question that jump-starts writers' imaginations. When the ten minutes are up, take a brief break.

Step 2: Read what you've written, and underline or highlight any phrases that excite you or pique your interest. Set the timer to 20 minutes. Now 'freewrite' about the underlined phrases. Let your imagination interpret them. Your thought journey may circle around the original prompt, or lead in new directions - either is fine. You can also ask yourself: How might this fit into a short story? How might this expand into a novel? How would this scenario play out in the fictional world I've created for my previous books? What would my series characters think about this situation, and how would they respond? How could this be even worse? What excites me about this prompt? What experience does this remind me of? How does this relate to my job, my ambitions, my dilemmas, my childhood, my relationships, people I used to know? Which aspects arouse my emotions, and why? And of course, that Open-Sesame question: What if...?

I suggest 'freewriting' about several prompts - perhaps one every day - before you decide which idea to develop into a work of fiction. One of them may visit you in your dreams at night, or make your body tingle all over whenever you think of it. That's the one to choose. Start building a plot for it. Save the others so you can use them for future projects.

When reading the prompts, or when jotting down your spontaneous thoughts during Step 1, you may remember having read a story that deals with a similar topic, or wonder what happens if many writers use the same prompt. Don't worry about this. There are few completely new ideas in speculative fiction. I doubt any book exists that doesn't include some previously-used components.

Indeed, many great works of horror fiction use the same basic premises to evoke primordial fears.

The key is to plant the idea seed into the fertile soil of your own imagination. What makes the story unique is the way you interpret the prompt, the context you place it in, and your individual author voice.

This method works well for getting creative juices flowing, for breaking through creative blocks, and for starting a new project.

The prompts in this collection work for all kinds of horror fiction - Psychological, Erotic, Splatterpunk and more - though not every prompt will suit every sub-genre. If you interpret the prompts freely, you can also apply them to related genres like Dark Fantasy, Steampunk and Thrillers.

If you're in the middle of a novel, this collection is less suitable. You may find my book *Mid-Novel Writing Prompts* (Writer's Craft #23) more helpful.

I'm writing in British English, with British spelling, grammar and punctuation. I've used the gender pronouns randomly, switching between 'she' and 'he'. Some of the prompts in this book overlap with suggestions I've offered in *Writing Scary Scenes* (Writer's Craft #2) and *Writing Dark Stories* (Writer's Craft #6).

Now let's get started. Do you have the timer set and the pen at hand? Ready... go!

Rayne Hall

HORROR WRITING PROMPT #1

An evil villain has a strict code of honour and ethics. What rule might he abide by, and in what terrible way does he make the issue fit the rule?

Ideas you can use:

Invent a rule that seems honourable. Then imagine how an evil person might interpret it.

Here are some examples:

"Don't kill." (= Get your minions to do the killing for you.)

"Never hurt an animal." (= Hurting a human is OK.)

"Never speak a lie." (= Put it in writing instead.)

"Never hurt someone over the age of seventy." (= Get your hands on that crone before she reaches that birthday.)

"Never harm a child under twelve." (= Snatch that eleven-year-old and keep him prisoner until his birthday.)

"Never attack another magician." (= Attack his helpless wife instead.)

"Never harm a virgin." (= Ensure she's no longer a virgin.)

_____

_____

_____

_____

_____

_____

HORROR WRITING PROMPT #2

A character accidentally maims or kills someone. That person (or their surviving spouse/parent/friend) seeks vengeance, and nothing will stop her.

Ideas you can use:

What kind of accident was it? A car crash? An explosion in the laboratory? A bodyguard or tour guide not paying attention at the critical moment?

How long ago did this happen?

Was it the character's fault? For a powerful story, consider making it partly bad luck, partly the character's fault. Perhaps the character had been drinking alcohol that evening, and although he wasn't drunk, his reaction speed was impaired. Or perhaps he had deliberately led his charge into a dangerous situation to scare her or teach her a lesson. Maybe he was busy flirting with a female he fancied, and didn't pay attention to what the other tour group members were doing.

Does the vengeance-seeker generally have an obsessive personality, or does she obsess only about this issue? You can add depth to the story if the vengeance-seeker herself contributed in some small way to the accident. Perhaps she skimped on buying the proper safety equipment for her child, or maybe she insisted on her spouse joining the expedition. This will allow you to add a layer of suppressed guilt to that character's personality and motivation.

Does the character still remember the event? How? Is it something he feels guilty for every day of his life, something he has long forgotten, or a memory he quickly suppresses whenever it comes to his mind?

How does the character first realise that the person is after him to seek vengeance?

What is the vengeance-seeker's aim? Does she seek to kill the perpetrator, cripple him, make him suffer? Perhaps her child fell into the ravine, and now she wants to throw the negligent tour guide into the same abyss. Maybe she lost both legs in the car crash, and now she wants the drunk driver to lose his legs, too.

How does she go about this? Does she infiltrate his staff, hire assassins, lure him to a remote location?

What if she doesn't target the perpetrator, but someone the perpetrator loves? Perhaps her ten-year-old son was eaten by alligators because of the tour guide's negligence. She postponed her vengeance until the tour guide had a son himself - and now she's determined to feed that child to the alligators.

How does the character react? Does he take the danger seriously at first, or does he laugh it off until he realises she's in earnest? Does he try to reason with her? Offer financial compensation? Hire lawyers or bodyguards? Flee?

Does he tell other people, or keep it secret? What if he can't tell his spouse what really happened that night, and therefore can't tell her about the present danger?

_____

_____

_____

_____

_____

_____

_____

_____

_____

_____

HORROR WRITING PROMPT #3

Who is this woman? What terrible suffering is inflicted on her... or what terrible suffering does she inflict on others? Why?

Art by Biljana Isevic. Copyright Rayne Hall.

Ideas you can use:

You can make this character the hero or the villain of your story. Look at her motivation.

Why does she do what she does? For whom does she do it?

Who is her main opponent?

What strengths and resources does she have to draw on?

HORROR WRITING PROMPT #4

A character plots to bring about the downfall of another character. He is so focused on this that he neglects to see the bigger picture of what is going on.

Ideas you can use:

This scenario can form part of a novel plot. It also works well as the main premise of a short story.

Where does this story play out? Is the character scheming to bring down a business competitor, a rival for job promotion, a love rival, a corrupt politician, the heir to the throne, or an unfaithful ex?

How does he go about this? What is at stake for each of the characters?

What is going on that he does not realise?

To give this story depth, explore several facets of scheming and disloyalty. For example, while the character is plotting to bring down the other character, his own supposedly loyal supporter is scheming against him.

_____

_____

_____

_____

_____

_____

_____

_____

_____

HORROR WRITING PROMPT #5

Which story scared you most when you were a child? Use the scariest part of this story in a new context.

Ideas you can use:

What was so scary about that story, or about that scene? Identify the detail that disturbed you most and sent your imagination spinning.

How might this play out in a different setting, or a different society? For example, if the story featured a princess in a castle, you might write about a famous pop star in a penthouse.

Change the characters. Instead of a child protagonist, create an adult hero. If the victim was female and the villain was male, change the genders around.

What events might lead to that scary situation? How might the situation be resolved?

_____

_____

_____

_____

_____

_____

_____

_____

_____

_____

_____

HORROR WRITING PROMPT #6

A character is obsessed with hunting down an evil person or monster. He doesn't listen to the pleas of a loved one who wants him to stop.

Ideas you can use:

What is this monster he needs to hunt? A serial killer, a dragon, a rabid tiger, a werewolf, a vampire, a traitor to the country?

Why does he need to hunt this monster? What drives his obsession? Perhaps the monster has killed someone he loved, and he wants revenge. What if he is motivated by religious fanaticism?

Who wants him to stop? His lover, spouse, parent, child, colleague (co-worker), team mate? Why does this person want him to give up the hunt? How does she try to persuade him?

Make the hunt as difficult and dangerous as possible to create excitement. Perhaps the character nearly dies in the pursuit but prevails.

How does it end? Does the character win, or the monster?

With this type of story, a double ending can work well: the character wins... but it's a short-term victory. Perhaps the slaughtered monster has a mate that is now out for revenge.

You can give the ending poignancy by letting the character win and then realise that his victory has cost him everything. Perhaps he defeats the monster, takes a trophy, and looks forward to basking in the honour and glory. But first, he just wants to go home, spend time with his lover/spouse/child and make it up to them for his previous neglect. When he arrives home, he finds the killer/monster has ravaged his family. While searching for the monster, he had left his family unprotected, and they fell prey. The trophy in his hands has become meaningless.

Another direction you can take the story is that the loved one wants him to give up the hunt because she knows the character himself is the evil monster. He doesn't realise this until the end of the story. This interpretation works well for psychological horror.

HORROR WRITING PROMPT #7

Imagine meeting this person in a dark street. What do you do?

Art by Erica Syverson. Copyright Rayne Hall.

Ideas you can use:

Is this person male, female or androgynous? What does he want? Is he after your blood - or something else altogether? What if he wants information or assistance?

Do you recognise him? Is he someone you know? Does he know you?

Is this an unexpected encounter, or an arranged meeting?

Will you give him what he wants? Or do you try to talk him out of it? Do you fight to defend yourself? Scream for help? Flee?

HORROR WRITING PROMPT #8

A character devotes herself to fighting evil, and brings great personal sacrifices for the greater good. After she triumphs, she realises that what she thought was evil was really good, and the supposed good was the true evil.

Ideas you can use:

What is the evil she wants to destroy? It is probably connected to an ideology, perhaps social, political or religious.

Why does she believe in her cause so much? How was she indoctrinated? People often fall for cults, false prophets, ideologies, radical religions and extreme political movements because they perceive a lack of structure and meaning in their own lives.

What sacrifices does she bring? Make them heart-wrenching. She denounces her mother, breaks up with her fiancé, assassinates her best friend. For best effect, make each sacrifice more terrible than the one before.

Let your character achieve a major triumph before she realises the truth: Her mother, her fiancé, her friend, were right. She had been blinded by her fanaticism. Those people she had deserted and killed had been wiser and fairer than her.

In a short story, she may actually defeat and eradicate the 'evil' she set out to destroy, and the story ends with her realisation that she was wrong.

In a novel, she may deal her opponent a devastating blow that cripples him without destroying him, forcing him underground. Once she realises that the opponent was the true hero - which happens about midway into the novel - she changes sides. Now she has to fight on the former enemy's side, struggle for secret survival, and suffer the consequences of the blow she dealt him. But first she has to convince him that she is on his side now - and after what she has done, he won't easily give his trust.

_____

_____

_____

_____

_____

_____

_____

_____

_____

_____

_____

_____

_____

_____

_____

_____

_____

_____

HORROR WRITING PROMPT #9

A danger threatens the community. Only one person can defeat the menace.

Ideas you can use:

For the reader, the story will probably be most exciting if you write it from the point of view (perspective) of that person. However, you can also write it from the PoV of someone who tries to persuade that person, or of the attacker who knows he has only one potential opponent.

What is the danger? It could be a mythical monster or an evil human.

Why is this person the only one who can save the community? Perhaps she possesses a rare skill or experience. For example, she used to be a lion-tamer or a circus acrobat, or maybe she once worked as the evil villain's personal assistant. Maybe something about her DNA marks her out.

She might also have a disability that becomes an ability in this context. For example, if the evil force has turned everything to total darkness, most people will be helpless and struggle to orient themselves, but a woman who was born blind will not be handicapped at all.

The rescuer is probably reluctant to get involved. Why? Perhaps she doesn't want to come out of retirement or has sworn an oath never to take up arms again. Perhaps the fight involves a conflict of loyalties, pitching her against her parents' tribe.

What persuades her to champion the defence after all?

How does she fight?

For dramatic structure, it is best if she fails in her first and second attempt. Then she learns something important, grows as a character, and changes tactics drastically. She tries again, and this time, in a gut-wrenching final confrontation, she wins.

HORROR WRITING PROMPT #10

How did those heads get up there?

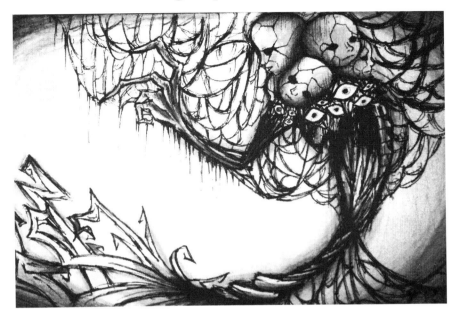

Art by WhiteNoiseGhost. Copyright Rayne Hall.

Ideas you can use:

Are they caught in an organic web, or in a man-made structure? Is this a tree, a plant or an organism that holds them?

What brought them there? A mistake, a curse, magic, vengeance?

Are the heads alive or dead? Can they communicate?

Is there a chance of rescue?

_____

_____

_____

HORROR WRITING PROMPT #11

People can increase their own life span by taking 'life units' from someone else.

Ideas you can use:

Is this exchange voluntary - perhaps a matter of honour, loyalty, love or payment? What makes this so terrible? What if the family or the community exerts enormous pressure on people to 'volunteer'? For example, anyone over the age of forty gets shamed if he doesn't give his life to someone younger than himself.

Or is it enforced? Perhaps serfs are expected to give a share of their lifespans to their masters, women to their husbands, prisoners of war to their conquerors, criminals to public resources?

What if a character can no longer trust those close to him, for fear that they are trying to take his 'life units'? What if the distrust ruins his marriage, his team, his family?

What if a character has to flee for his life and hide, because others are after his 'life units'?

Can anyone obtain 'life units' from anyone else, or does it work only between close relatives or members of the same ethnic group?

What if trade is illegal but flourishing? Do brokers arrange deals?

What if there are fund raising drives - collecting donations not of money, but of 'life units'?

Is there a limit to how many 'life units' a person can give?

How is the transfer carried out - with a magic ritual under the full moon, or a surgical procedure in a hospital?

Does the quality of life the recipient obtains depend on the donor's health? What if health problems are passed on - arthritis, AIDS, drug addiction?

Rayne Hall

HORROR WRITING PROMPT #12

Invaders rob locals of parts of their physical bodies.

Ideas you can use:

Who are the invaders? Members of a different tribe? Extra-terrestrials? Vampires? Uninvited missionaries? A conquering army?

What body parts do they take, and for what purpose? Hair for wig-making? Teeth to make dentures? Kidneys for organ transplants? Fingernails for magic rituals? Legs for anatomical studies?

How are the donors coerced? Do they survive the extraction?

What if they resist?

_____

_____

_____

_____

_____

_____

_____

_____

_____

_____

_____

_____

_____

HORROR WRITING PROMPT #13

Extreme climate change makes survival almost impossible.

Ideas you can use:

Is the climate change permanent? If yes, what caused it - the damage to the ozone layer or the impact of a colliding comet tilting the earth's axis?

Are people aware that the change is permanent, or do they hope it's a temporary condition that will right itself?

How does the climate/weather/temperature change? Does it get colder, hotter, wetter, dryer? Do the sea levels rise or the rivers dry out? The more extreme the new climate, the more extreme will people's actions become, so consider raising or dropping the temperature by thirty degrees, or taking away all the rivers or forests.

What are the consequences? Do more insects hatch because their larvae didn't die in the cold? Do certain predators become near extinct, so their previous prey multiplies and spreads? What if a previously harmless animal species loses its accustomed food, and turns savage?

How do people adapt to the changed weather? How do they react to the change in the ecosystem?

What do they need to do to survive that they would previously not have considered?

How about cannibalism? Do they hunt other humans for food? Are there moral restrictions, e.g. not to slaughter children, pregnant women, or members of one's own family?

When faced with extreme hardship and resources don't stretch to keep everyone alive, many societies cast out their weak members - the old, sick, disabled or very young. Sometimes, it's a matter of honour for old people to sacrifice themselves so the young members of the tribe can survive, for example, by walking out into the cold or by drowning themselves in the sea. At other times, someone in power orders the rounding up and culling of unwanted people.

What if officials declare that all prisoners must be executed, all foreigners must be drowned, or all hospital patients must be euthanised?

What if this is not an official decree, but the act of a gang of individuals who take the law into their own hands? They may storm the hospital or the prison to kill the inmates, or they may assassinate everyone who doesn't belong to their ethnic group.

Consider increasing the horror of the situation gradually, starting with relatively small problems (which of course seem big at the time) and building up to people dying, e.g. from harmful rays of the sun because the ozone layer is damaged, or from suffocation due to lack of oxygen.

_____

_____

_____

_____

_____

_____

_____

_____

_____

_____

_____

HORROR WRITING PROMPT #14

Look at this picture. What happened?

Art by Michelle Greaves. Copyright Rayne Hall.

Ideas you can use:

Is this a werewolf-woman who has changed into her animal form so suddenly that she didn't have the chance to take off her dress and jewellery first?

Is it a wolf hiding from hunters by seeking refuge in a human home?

Has the wolf just eaten the woman to whom these clothes belong?

What if this wolf has just eaten the grandmother, and Little Red Riding Hood is knocking at the door?

What will happen next?

HORROR WRITING PROMPT #15

A character hears about a danger, mocks it as superstition, and sets out to prove it's not real.

Ideas you can use:

What is this danger? How about an ancient religion, a haunted room, a mysterious savage beast roaming the moor?

To build tension, let him enter the danger zone and initially find what he believes is evidence that he is right. But then things get stranger and stranger, and he finds himself in real danger. He fights against the threat, narrowly getting away with his life. He relaxes for a moment - and discovers that the danger is even worse than supposed.

To add another dimension to this story, and to facilitate dialogue, consider giving him a companion. This could be a friend, lover, colleague, servant or team mate. The companion is more cautious than he, and reluctant to take the risk, but joins him out of loyalty.

Try to show character growth in this story. The main character emerges a wiser person.

A natural ending for this type of story is that after a terrible ordeal, the character finally defeats the threat. He has escaped, but will never mock superstition again.

You can add poignancy if he achieved the victory at a price. Perhaps his loyal companion is dead, crippled or insane.

HORROR WRITING PROMPT #16

A character tries to overcome a personal weakness, and goes too far.

Ideas you can use:

What is this personal weakness? How about prejudice, cowardice, substance addiction?

Here is a suggestion how you might structure this story. The character fights against her habits (and instincts), and fails. She tries again, fails again. She tries once more, making a heroic effort, and succeeds.

The true horror lies in the ending. She realises, too late, that in this instance she should have listened to her instincts after all. She has made herself an easy victim.

You can end the story with her grasping her stupidity and her imminent demise. This plot structure works well for a short story.

For a novel, it's probably better not to end here, but to make the realisation the story's 'Black Moment' and allow the character to rally her strength for the book's climax.

_____

_____

_____

_____

_____

_____

_____

HORROR WRITING PROMPT #17

Where is this man trying to go or escaping from?

Photo: Creative Commons Stock Photos. Photographer unspecified.

Ideas you can use:

Is he trying to escape from a prison or internment camp?

Does he attempt to break into a place and burgle it?

Is he fleeing from people who want him dead?

Maybe he is a private investigator, a cop, or an urban explorer? Could he be a vampire on the prowl?

What if a moment ago he was sitting at his desk in the office or walking his dog in the park, and suddenly he finds himself in this environment? How might this have come about?

Has the light in the background just come on? Is it a movement-sensing lamp? If yes, does this mean he'll be discovered?

Write the story from his point-of-view.

Horror Writing Prompts

HORROR WRITING PROMPT #18

Do you have a recurring nightmare, or does a disturbing element feature in your dreams again and again? Weave a story around it.

Ideas you can use:

In your dreams, are you standing at an abyss, about to fall? Write a story in which a character stands on the edge of a cliff. Is a knife-wielding madman chasing you every night? Send him after a fictional character. Do your dreams trap you on a sinking ship? Put your characters into the same peril.

Focus on the most terrifying part of the dream. You can change the dream's details and outcome, but aim to convey the feeling.

Stories inspired by dreams are often very powerful (and successful) because they work with the force of your subconscious mind.

_____

_____

_____

_____

_____

_____

_____

_____

_____

_____

HORROR WRITING PROMPT #19

A character lands in a situation where she has only two options, and both are morally or ethically wrong. She must jettison one dearly held value to adhere to the other.

Ideas you can use:

Start by deciding what this person's most deeply held values are. The values may relate to her personal integrity, her religious faith, her family and loved ones, or her loyalty. Then pitch those values against each other, and create a scenario where she has to choose.

You can intensify this story by making her a righteous character, someone who demands the highest moral standards of herself and others. She tolerates neither sin nor lax ethics, and obsessively demands that others do the right thing at all times. Establish these personality traits at the beginning of the story. However, take care not to make her a bigot or a prig.

_____

_____

_____

_____

_____

_____

_____

_____

_____

_____

HORROR WRITING PROMPT #20

This man poses a threat. To whom, and why?

Photo by Tookapic/Pexels. Copyright Tookapic.

Ideas you can use:

Is this man a worker, guarding a site against intruders?

Is he an enforcer, about to smash the legs of a defaulter or dissident?

Is he stopping cars at night to threaten the passengers?

Is he a refugee from the justice system, ready to fight for his freedom?

_____

_____

_____

HORROR WRITING PROMPT #21

In a location where rooms and flats to rent are scarce, a character urgently needs somewhere to stay. At last, she finds an acceptable arrangement... and regrets it soon after she moves in.

Ideas you can use:

Where might your story be set? How about a city like Paris, New York or London where rentals are hard to find and prohibitively expensive? Or maybe it's in an exclusive resort or gated community where people of the wrong skin colour or ex-convicts are not welcome.

What's wrong with the place? Is it haunted by a chain-rattling ghost or infested with monstrous bed bugs? Does a resident spirit demand a human sacrifice every winter solstice, and that's why the regular tenant was keen to sublet the flat for the season? Do the flatmates indulge in criminal activities and force her to provide them with false alibis? Is the neighbour in the flat above a sadistic killer who tortures his victims, and the tenant has to listen to the agonised cries every night?

To make the character's actions plausible, let her know that the arrangement has a catch. Perhaps the landlord warns her in advance that the upstairs neighbour can be noisy, or the flatmates tell her that they are a bit of a wild bunch.

Let her grasp the horror only gradually, and when she finally realises the full extent, it's too late because she has already become an accomplice or victim.

HORROR WRITING PROMPT #22

A sadistic villain makes a victim choose: either she will be mutilated or someone she loves will.

Ideas you can use:

How does this situation come about? Is it the vengeance of an individual, or a legal penalty?

What kind of mutilation? Will the person be blinded, castrated, have their right hand cut off?

Who is the loved one: her husband, her mother, her child?

To create tension and churn the reader's heart, make the choice as difficult as possible. For example, she may want to protect her child at all costs - but without her hands, she won't be able to earn a living to feed it.

Keep the reader uncertain of the outcome of her choice. For example, she may decide to sacrifice herself for her lover - but then she learns that he betrayed her. Perhaps it was he who revealed her whereabouts to the villain's henchmen, so that they would spare his life.

Finish the short story soon after the character makes her choice. You can leave it open whether or not her decision was the right one. For added drama, show a final interaction between her and the loved one. That person's response may suggest that she did, or didn't, make the right choice.

In a novel, the plot can continue. Now she needs to continue her life and the pursuit of her goal, either crippled by the loss of her limb or burdened by guilt.

_____

_____

_____

HORROR WRITING PROMPT #23

A community gets isolated from the outside world.

Ideas you can use:

How does the community get isolated? Is there a flood, a climate change, a siege? Perhaps these people live in a remote place already, but normally they can travel and have communications with the outside world. They could live in a clearing in the rainforest or on an island in the ocean.

Maybe they chose to isolate themselves temporarily from the rest of the world, for example, for a trek across the desert or for a spiritual retreat in a mountain monastery, but something happens (perhaps a war, or a climate catastrophe) and the world forgets about their existence. Perhaps refugees are hiding in a remote location until the wave of religious persecution passes or their crimes come under the statute of limitations, and in the meantime, they rely on a trusted person to provide them with supplies and information - and when that person dies, nobody knows of their existence.

You can write about a small community - just a family perhaps, or members of an expedition - or a large one, such as a town or a college.

To build tension, let them realise their predicament gradually.

What will they do to break out of their isolation?

What tensions and conflicts arise between members of the community? They probably got on reasonably well while the isolation was voluntary or temporary. But when they realise that they're stuck together for a long time or forever, tensions and conflicts will escalate. They may also fight about resources and jostle for power.

HORROR WRITING PROMPT #24

Write about this doll.

Photo by Desertrose7/Pixabay. Copyright Desertrose7

Ideas you can use:

Who made this doll? Who clothed it?

Who owns it now? A child? An adult for whom it represents a fond (or dark) memory of childhood? Is it a family heirloom?

Who owned the doll previously?

Is the doll sentient? What emotions does it have? Can it think, plan, scheme? Is it good or evil? What does it want?

_____

_____

_____

HORROR WRITING PROMPT #25

A character has never thought to pursue a certain dangerous venture - until someone else warns him persistently not to try it. Now his interest is piqued.

Ideas you can use:

What is this venture? An expedition, exploration, scientific experiment?

Why is it so dangerous?

Who is the person who warns the character? A spouse, colleague, subordinate, sibling, friend?

Why does the character act against that person's advice? Is it curiosity, pride, stubbornness? Embed this reaction in the character's personality profile.

The venture turns out to be far more difficult than the character thought. Add unexpected hazards to build the danger.

The person who warned him needs to play a further role in the plot. Does she accompany him on the expedition? Or perhaps she serves as his link to the outside world, receiving and relaying his messages? Or does she shut off all contact with him because he didn't listen to her?

Does she greet him on his return? Does his success convince her that he is strong, brave and capable, a better man than she thought, so she finally accepts his proposal? Or does his insistence on the foolhardy adventure show him to be irresponsible, so she breaks off their engagement?

If you want a dark twist, consider this: confronting the danger, the character nearly dies when his equipment fails, but escapes. If only he can reach/contact his spouse/colleague/friend/team mate/the helpline/the escape route he'll be safe. But she's not at the arranged meeting place/hasn't provided the support she promised. Worse, she has destroyed the shelter/disabled the helpline/blocked the escape route. Belatedly, the character realises the spouse/colleague/friend wants him to die, has set him up, needled him into the venture and prepared the trap.

You can end the story there, or you can continue with a double twist: bereft of support and illusions, he fights against the menace, and wins. The traitor falls into the trap she laid for him. He couldn't save her even if he nobly wanted to, because she has destroyed the means of rescue.

_____

_____

_____

_____

_____

_____

_____

_____

_____

_____

_____

_____

_____

_____

_____

HORROR WRITING PROMPT #26

A character wants to belong to a group, and works to convince members that he is worthy. Too late he realises what this group is really about.

Ideas you can use:

What kind of group is it? Think of an exclusive club, a religious cult, an erotic scene, an inner-city gang, the in-crowd in the local pub, the popular girls in school, a secret society, keepers of a secret.

Perhaps he is motivated by curiosity first, but then gets a taste of it and wants more. What makes membership so attractive? What does this group offer that he can't get elsewhere?

He works hard to convince members that he is worthy. How?

He is granted basic initiation and a second experience that's so thrilling that he is completely hooked. He will do what it takes to get accepted to the inner circle and enjoy the pleasures to the full. At this stage, make the reader feel the character's urgent desire to belong, but also plant hints that something else is going on.

When he's finally taken to the inner circle and involved in his third experience, he realises it is evil. What he thought of as desirable pleasure or a noble cause is a horrific exploitation of victims. But at this stage it is too late to back out.

Why is it too late? Perhaps he has committed crimes, or witnessed so much that the gang can't let him live.

Will he go ahead? Or will he back out and pay the price?

You can develop the ending in several ways. Each is terrible in its own way:

   a. You can end the story with his realisation, leaving it open about what he will do.

b. His conscience wins. Rather than aid evil, he sacrifices himself.

c. He decides to go ahead and enjoy the thrills as a full member of the group.

This will make a complete short story.

For a novel, the realisation of what he got himself into is probably only the first part of the plot (between one and two thirds into the book). The novel will then show how he fights against the power the cult has over him and others.

HORROR WRITING PROMPT #27

What is this place, and why would someone come here?

Art by Biljana Isevic. Copyright Rayne Hall.

Ideas you can use:

What emotion does this picture evoke in you? Loneliness? Fear? Curiosity? Aim to let the reader experience the same feeling, perhaps by making it the main character's dominant emotion.

What place is this? Is it on Earth, on a distant planet, or in a different reality? Is it the Underworld, or a place from mythology?

Why and how would someone go there? Is she part of this - perhaps one of the figures in the ritual on the left? Or is she there by stealth, hiding to watch the goings-on? Is she there by choice, or was she dragged there as an unwilling participant to the ritual? What if everyone enters this place after death, before passing on to their final destiny?

Will she get away again? Does anyone ever leave this place alive?

What sounds are in this place? What smells?

What are the eyes on the right?

HORROR WRITING PROMPT #28

A newly-dead person rises because he has unfinished business to conclude.

Ideas you can use:

How does he rise - as a ghost, a zombie, a vampire, or something else?

Where does he rise from - his bed, his coffin, the funeral pyre?

What unfinished business does he have to conclude - wreaking vengeance, fulfilling a promise, begging forgiveness, get his daughter married, punish his murderer, mending a wrong he has done?

Being undead requires some adjustment. You can create humour here, and it's up to you if you want to make the story funny or just add a little black humour.

He is determined to do whatever it takes to accomplish his mission. What obstacles does he encounter?

Let him grow as a person. He learns/understands/realises something he hadn't been aware of. About what? Perhaps about himself, his spouse, his murderer, his death, his own guilt, his current state?

When he finally gets the chance to carry out his plan, will he do it? Or will he change his mind and desist? Why?

The story probably ends with his return to the coffin (or funeral pyre) and permanent death.

_____

_____

_____

_____

HORROR WRITING PROMPT #29

What does this character want?

Art by Jamie Chapman. Copyright Rayne Hall.

Ideas you can use:

Is this man about to commit an atrocity?

Is he seeking to escape?

Is he investigating a strange noise in the castle?

What if he is about to witness something horrendous?

Perhaps he is going to feed a prisoner or pass on his lord's order for the captive's execution?

HORROR WRITING PROMPT #30

A character who has an irrational fear tries to overcome it.

Ideas you can use:

What is she frightened of? A person, a type of people, an animal species, an object? Her boss? Drug dealers? Hispanics? Clowns? Horses? Rabbits? Butterflies? Motor cars? Rubber bands? Thermos flasks? The grandfather clock in the living room?

You can give the story a sense of authenticity if you choose something that frightens you or gives you the creeps as inspiration.

The character always takes drastic precautions against this perceived threat. What precautions are these?

At last, she tries to overcome her irrational fears. How does she do this? Does she get psychotherapy, does she hypnotise herself, does she practice positive self-talk? (You may want to research treatment methods for phobias and irrational fears, to give your story realism.)

In this, she is probably successful. She acknowledges that her fears are irrational, that the person/animal/object is harmless. She realises that it was her own unhealthy imagination that led her into this obsession.

She dismantles her defences.

Now the person/animal/object attacks. The threat - or an aspect of it - was real. By talking herself out of her fear, she suppressed her healthy instincts and common-sense caution.

If you're writing a short story, you can end it with the character's insight and imminent demise.

With a novel, these events are probably just part of a bigger plot, and the character survives.

HORROR WRITING PROMPT #31

What is this creature?

Art by Geralt/Pixabay. Copyright: Geralt.

Ideas you can use:

Where does this creature come from? What does it want? Who sent it?

Does it have free will, or does it purely follow orders?

Where does it live?

How can it harm humans?

How can it be defeated?

Who encounters this creature? Why?

Rayne Hall

HORROR WRITING PROMPT #32

An innocent observes seemingly harmless actions. But the reader understands that there is something sinister going on that the innocent doesn't understand.

Ideas you can use:

Who is this innocent? A child? A newcomer to the community?

What do the people really do?

What does the innocent think they do?

Are they aware that they are being watched? If yes, do they explain their actions? Why does the innocent believe them?

Does the innocent suspect anything at all? You can create tension if the innocent has flashes of suspicion but suppresses them.

_____

_____

_____

_____

_____

_____

_____

_____

_____

_____

HORROR WRITING PROMPT #33

A freelancer gets hired to create a memorial for a client's dead spouse. Too late, the freelancer realises what exactly his client has in mind, and that this involves the freelancer's death.

Ideas you can use:

What kind of freelance work does he do? Is he an architect, a painter, a composer? Consider writing about a field about which you are knowledgeable, because this will give your story plausibility and authenticity and cut down on research.

Who is the client? Although he will be the antagonist of this piece, you can give the story depth by making him a sympathetic character, at least in part. Perhaps his grief has affected his rational judgement and his compassion. Grief may even have driven him insane.

What kind of monument does the freelancer create? What makes this assignment so attractive to the freelancer? In what way does it appeal to his artistic sense and creativity?

When does the freelancer first suspect that there's something the client hasn't told him? What other cues are there? How does he react - does he suppress his first suspicions or seek clarification and reassurance?

How does the story end? Does the freelancer survive? Does the client?

_____

_____

_____

_____

HORROR WRITING PROMPT #34

A kraken (giant sea monster) attacks humans.

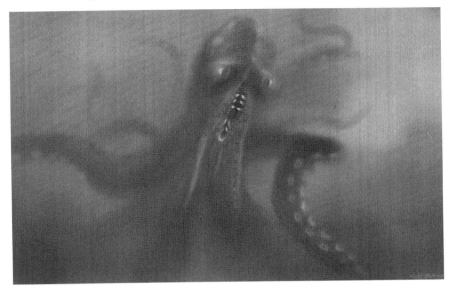

Art by Biljana Isevic. Copyright Rayne Hall.

Ideas you can use:

Legends of kraken - either several monsters or one single creature of enormous size - go back hundreds of years. They may have been based on real sightings of real ocean creatures, probably a giant octopus or a giant squid.

Squid and octopuses can reach enormous sizes in nature, and it is plausible that some grow even larger. The deep seas are home to life forms not yet discovered and classified, and the water can support large bodies. You may want to search online for 'giant octopus sightings' or 'giant squid' and use the results for inspiration.

Many legends tell of kraken reaching out with tentacles to grab and capsize boats. Others say the kraken snatches individual humans from the deck of a ship.

The most common location of the mythical creature is in the waters of the Scandinavian seas. However, sightings have also been reported in other parts of the world, so you can set your story anywhere.

What if a kraken lives not in the sea, but in a local lake, loch or pond? How did it get there? If the lake is deep and natural, the creature (or its ancestors) have lived there since prehistoric times when the body of water was still connected to the sea.

What makes the kraken rise now? What if it has been disturbed by water pollution or underwater explosions?

Why does it attack humans? Does it seek to eradicate humankind, to feed itself (or its offspring), or to exact vengeance for the killing of its mate?

What it if preys on fishing boats, on the navy fleet stationed nearby, or on the seashore close to the children's bathing area?

What if nations use krakens as war animals, provoking it into sinking the enemy fleet?

_____

_____

_____

_____

_____

_____

_____

_____

_____

_____

_____

HORROR WRITING PROMPT #35

Tell a fairy tale from the perspective of the villain.

Ideas you can use:

Think back to the fairy tales you heard when you were a child. Choose one in which the villain (the wicked witch or evil stepmother, perhaps) comes to a terrible end, suffering just punishment for her deeds.

Now consider: what if the villain was innocent? What if she was set up or framed? What if the fairy tale version you heard was the result of propaganda?

What if Prince Charming was really evil, and arranged it so that the kindly witch got the blame for his deeds?

Think especially about what motivates the characters. What if the supposed villain was not just a good character, but a noble one, sacrificing herself to save someone else?

You can tell the story with the style and setting of a fairy tale, or you can present it as modern fiction with a contemporary setting.

The reader's horror will gradually mount as they recognise the story and realise that this noble character is headed for the gruesome fate.

At the end of this book, I'm including a story I wrote based on this idea, so you can see how it can work.

_____

_____

_____

_____

Rayne Hall

HORROR WRITING PROMPT #36

Where does this animal come from? What does it do?

Art by Michelle Greaves. Copyright Rayne Hall.

Ideas you can use:

Does it bite humans? Does it have a poisonous sting? Does it carry diseases?

What if eggs arrived in travellers' luggage from an exotic country, and hatched?

Is it one of a kind, or is there a whole swarm of these creatures?

How quickly do they multiply?

What do they feed on?

How can it be exterminated? For plot purposes, you may want to make it immune to pesticides and sonic repellents.

HORROR WRITING PROMPT #37

A character fights an unusual addiction.

Ideas you can use:

What is this character addicted to? Torturing victims? Drinking human blood fresh from the body?

Why does he want to stop? What does he do to curb his addiction?

Who knows of his addiction?

How does it feel to desperately need what he is addicted to? You may want to research how other addicts (drug users, alcoholics) experience their addiction.

You can write the story from the perspective of the addict, a victim, or someone who tries to stop him.

_____

_____

_____

_____

_____

_____

_____

_____

_____

_____

HORROR WRITING PROMPT #38

Write a story about this spider, from the point-of-view of a person who fears spiders.

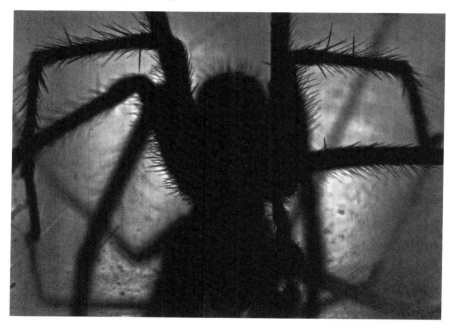

Photo: Creative Commons Stock Photos. (Photographer not specified.)

Ideas you can use:

Where does the person encounter the spider?

How big is it? Describe its appearance, size and movements creatively.

How does it make him feel? Describe the physical sensations he experiences when he sees the beast.

What's his fear of spiders like? Do spiders give him the creeps, or does he have arachnophobia? Has he had a horrifying encounter with a spider that scared him for life?

How does he react to this spider? Does he screech, scream, run away, faint or try to kill it?

Is the spider dangerous?

Is there just one spider, or are there several?

What if someone knows of the character's phobia, and deliberately planted the spider in his room?

What if an evil villain locks an arachnophobic person into a spider-filled cell?

_____

_____

_____

_____

_____

_____

_____

_____

_____

_____

_____

_____

_____

_____

HORROR WRITING PROMPT #39

A character gets immured (bricked up alive).

Ideas you can use:

This is a particularly cruel, slow method of death by dehydration and starvation. Imagine the days of fear, desperation, hope and agony.

Immurement was a legal punishment in some historical periods. For example, in Ancient Rome, a vestal virgin who broke her vow of chastity was sealed in a subterraneous chamber. In the German town of Augsburg in 1409, priests found guilty of pederasty (sexual intercourse with boys) were locked into a wooden casket hung up in a tower. Until the early 20th century, robbers in Persia were cemented into pillars with just a little air allowed to penetrate.

In times of war, conquerors sometimes used immurement as mass punishment for those who resisted the occupation.

Personal vengeance is another reason for immurement, and there are many examples in history and legend, especially in Indian mythology.

Another possibility is human sacrifice. For example, a living human may get walled into the foundations of a new public monument or defensive wall, in the believe that this will protect the building or shield the fortress against invasion. When a royal ruler dies, his retinue may get bricked up in his tomb.

You can write the story from the perspective of a person getting immured. Did they willingly risk the fate by breaking a law, knowing what the penalty would be if caught? Or are they a tyrant's hapless victims? Caution: putting yourself into the prisoner's mind can be a terrifying experience for the writer.

Alternatively, you can tell the story from the perspective of the person who orders the immurement or carries it out. Horrifying the reader by showing the madman's state of mind requires considerable skill, so this is not for beginner writers.

If you'd rather not describe the gruesome cruelty in graphic detail, consider writing a ghost story. A person who was bricked up alive hundreds of years ago now haunts the place.

_____

_____

_____

_____

_____

_____

_____

_____

_____

_____

_____

_____

_____

_____

_____

_____

_____

HORROR WRITING PROMPT #40

Write about this picture.

Photo by simonwijers/Pixabay. Copyright simonwijers.

Ideas you can use:

Who are these people? What are they doing?

Are they hiding? If so, why are their hands visible? Hiding from whom?

Are they hugging trees as part of a protest? If so, protest against what? Why don't they show their faces and bodies?

Are they drawing energy from trees? If so, why are the arms and fingers so tense?

_____

_____

_____

_____

_____

_____

_____

_____

_____

_____

_____

_____

_____

_____

_____

_____

_____

_____

_____

_____

_____

_____

_____

_____

_____

_____

_____

Rayne Hall

HORROR WRITING PROMPT #41

A person gets shrunk by another.

Ideas you can use:

This story will probably straddle the Horror and Fantasy genres.

Who shrinks whom? What is their relationship?

What is the motivation of the 'shrinker' - sadistic pleasure at another's suffering, vengeance, power?

For the strongest horror and tension, make the shrinking gradual. Let it happen over several hours or days.

Perhaps the 'shrinkee' doesn't realise immediately what's going on. Maybe she notices that her muscles are aching, or rejoices that she's finally lost weight when she steps on her bathroom scales. Then her shoes have a loose fit and she needs to adjust the height of her office chair. Gradually it dawns on her. Perhaps she feels worry and disbelief at first, later panic and terror.

What does she do while shrinking? She may plead with the 'shrinker' to reverse the process. Perhaps she tries to stop or reverse the process herself. What if she uses her miniscule size to inflict harm on the person who shrunk her? Or maybe she is focussed on survival - where can she live and be safe from predators?

How small does she shrink? Will she be the size of a child, a doll, a matchbox or a seed?

Describe the physical sensations of shrinking (does it hurt?), as well as the thoughts and emotions. Show size comparisons, for example, the kitten she held in her palm at the beginning of the story is now bigger than her, or the spiders she used to squash are now huge menacing monsters out to devour her.

Is she the only person who has shrunk, or are there others? If writing a novel, consider a community of shrunk people. For a short story, she can be the only one.

How does the shrinking happen? Does the 'shrinker' apply a scientific method or a magic spell?

Can it be reversed?

The ending can be happy (she gets restored to size, or finds happiness in a miniature life), unhappy (she gets devoured by a spider, or he keeps shrinking in all eternity), or open (she gets a chance to be restored to size, but will she take it? The miniature people develop a method to restore their size, but will it work?).

_____

_____

_____

_____

_____

_____

_____

_____

_____

_____

_____

_____

_____

_____

HORROR WRITING PROMPT #42

Filled with apprehension, a character walks along this corridor. Where to?

Photo: Creative Commons Stock Photos. (Photographer not specified.)

Ideas you can use:

Consider what kind of building this is, and what businesses, offices or laboratories might be housed here.

The character knows something bad is going to happen to him - but he probably does not know what exactly. Why does he go there despite his forebodings?

Describe the corridor in a way that makes the reader feel apprehensive with the character. Describe the light, the sounds of the character's steps on the floor, and creepy background noises.

_____

_____

_____

_____

_____

_____

_____

_____

_____

_____

_____

_____

_____

_____

_____

_____

HORROR WRITING PROMPT #43

Write about reincarnation: something terrible about a character's past life catches up with him.

Ideas you can use:

Does a person he harmed in a previous life pursue him for vengeance?

Did he inflict terrible harm on someone else in a past life, and now he has to suffer the same fate?

Does he immediately realise the past life connection and remember the details?

Does he believe in reincarnation?

What if he doesn't believe in reincarnation and doesn't remember what happened - but the vengeance-crazed person does?

What measures does he take to protect himself or to avert the fate?

_____

_____

_____

_____

_____

_____

_____

_____

_____

HORROR WRITING PROMPT #44

Write about a dangerous, painful or gruesome initiation ritual.

Ideas you can use:

Who gets initiated into what? Is there a single initiate, or a whole group?

Is the initiation into a gang, a religious cult, a political extremist group, a secret society, a trade?

What if the group appears benign, and the initiate realises belatedly, during the ritual, that it is evil?

What if a whole group gets initiated - a tribe, a family, a graduating class - and not everyone truly consents?

What does the initiation involve? Does the initiate do something, or is something done to him?

Must he carry out an action he abhors, such as torture an animal or kill someone? Did he know in advance that this would be expected of him, or does it take him by surprise?

If something is done to him, is this painful or dangerous? Does it involve some form of physical mutilation? Perhaps initiates get tattooed on a particularly sensitive body part, or have a toe removed without anaesthetic? Some initiation rituals involve the sexual organs, and may range from circumcision to castration.

_____

_____

_____

_____

HORROR WRITING PROMPT #45

Write about this boar.

Art by Michelle Greaves. Copyright Rayne Hall.

Ideas you can use:

Whom does this boar attack, and why?

Is a character trying to kill the boar? Perhaps the story takes place during a hunt?

What if the boar is a human in animal form, perhaps the result of a curse or magic spell? What if the character recognises a dead loved one by the eyes?

The story could be set in the present day or in a historical period.

_____

_____

_____

_____

_____

Horror Writing Prompts

_____

_____

_____

_____

_____

_____

_____

_____

_____

_____

_____

_____

_____

_____

_____

_____

_____

_____

_____

_____

HORROR WRITING PROMPT #46

A person arrives as a stranger in a new place where she is welcomed and honoured. Then she realises she is intended as a human sacrifice.

Ideas you can use:

Why does she travel to this place? Is she a holiday-maker, does she visit someone, or is she looking for work? Perhaps she is a refugee, an illegal immigrant, a development aid worker, an au pair or a runaway teenager?

What country, town or culture is she visiting? How long does she intend to stay? How much does she know about the place and its traditions?

Does she speak the language?

What's her first experience of being so warmly welcomed? What does she attribute this welcome to... local hospitality customs, her nationality, her bloodline, her skills?

When does she first begin to suspect the truth? Does the reader get an inkling of wrongness before the character does?

Once she realises that the people mean to sacrifice her, how does she try to escape this fate? How do the locals prevent it?

Let the character's and reader's fear mount gradually from apprehension and suspicion to disbelief, shock and terror.

HORROR WRITING PROMPT #47

Members of a society are required to kill each other as a matter of honour.

Ideas you can use:

Start by deciding what the custom and justification for these 'honour killings' is. What if young people, on reaching adulthood, are expected to kill their grandparents? What if husbands must kill unfaithful wives? What if the youngest son of each family must kill the oldest? What if parents must kill daughters who are not married by a certain age? What if families must kill gay relatives? What if couples are allowed to have a child only after proving that they have carried out a killing? What if the law stipulates the death penalty for certain crimes, with the execution carried out by their next of kin?

Then select the point of view. You can choose someone who does not wish to kill, or someone who doesn't want to be killed.

_____

_____

_____

_____

_____

_____

_____

_____

_____

_____

HORROR WRITING PROMPT #48

Why is this woman barefoot in the wood?

Photo: Creative Commons Stock Photos. (Photographer not specified.)

Ideas you can use:

Does she live nearby, and did she wake at night? Why did she leave her home without getting dressed and putting on shoes?

Perhaps she has been camping with friends, and coming out of the tent she sees something that disturbs her.

Is she a kidnap victim who has escaped her captors? Perhaps they took away her clothes and shoes. Why is she not running? Her pose seems tentative. If she has fled some distance through the woods, would not her feet and legs be scratched and bleeding?

HORROR WRITING PROMPT #49

A character has to pass a test to prove worthy of membership.

Ideas you can use:

What club/group/society/institution/cult does he want to join? Why?

What is so gruesome about the membership test? Does he have to do something terrible, or endure a cruel ordeal?

What if the test is rigged so he won't pass? Perhaps the group, or an individual, does not want him to become a member. Maybe they give him a map, survival tool or weapon, and he realises that it is false or malfunctioning and useless. Perhaps as part of the test he needs to spend the night in a remote or dangerous location, and after surviving the night, he discovers that they have abandoned him.

How long does it take him to realise the truth? What does he do now?

_____

_____

_____

_____

_____

_____

_____

_____

_____

HORROR WRITING PROMPT #50

Write about this person.

Art by Jamie Chapman. Copyright Rayne Hall.

Ideas you can use:

Is this a ghost? A zombie? A living person after prolonged abuse, illness or starvation?

What does this person want or need?

You can write the story from the perspective of this creature, or from that of someone who encounters it.

HORROR WRITING PROMPT #51

Two lovers have to fight each other to the death in a public event. Only one may live.

Ideas you can use:

What's the reason for this fight? Is this a religious ritual involving human sacrifice, or a public spectacle?

What if the fight is a form of public execution - if yes, for what? Adultery? Homosexuality? Mixed race relations?

Do they realise who their opponent is going to be, or is this a shocking surprise?

Will one try to sacrifice his life for his lover?

Reveal something about the other person and the relationship that the point-of-view character did not previously know.

Aim to give this story emotional impact.

_____

_____

_____

_____

_____

_____

_____

_____

_____

HORROR WRITING PROMPT #52

What happens in this empty train compartment?

Photo: Creative Commons Stock Photos. (Photographer not specified.)

Ideas you can use:

Why is the point-of-view character in this carriage? Is he travelling somewhere, or looking for someone or something?

Is the carriage really empty? Are there people sitting at the far end? Are they waiting for the character?

Will a guard or conductor enter it during the journey?

What if something bad happens, and the character can't use his mobile phone to call for help, because the train is going through a tunnel?

Horror Writing Prompts

HORROR WRITING PROMPT #53

A person creates something good, useful and innocuous - but the raw material is derived from human bodies.

Ideas you can use:

What is it she does or makes? Think of something not normally associated with horror. Perhaps she makes artists' paints or compost for her rose garden.

Does she need whole bodies, or only specific parts, such as ground-up teeth, eyes, livers or spinal fluid?

Does she use dead bodies? If yes, where does she obtain them?

Does she need living bodies? If yes, do the victims survive the procedure - minus their eyes or teeth? What if she keeps a prisoner from whom to extract one tooth at a time (perhaps without anaesthetic, since this would adversely affect the quality of the paint)?

How did she discover the properties of the human ingredient?

Why does the material have to be human rather than animal?

_____

_____

_____

_____

_____

_____

_____

_____

HORROR WRITING PROMPT #54

What did you fear when you were a child? Write a story about it.

Ideas you can use:

Did you think there was a monster under your bed or in your wardrobe?

Did the root cellar in your grandparent's home terrify you? Perhaps you had an inexplicable fear of a certain neighbour, or the house on the corner gave you the creeps.

Imagine that your fear was justified, that there really is a monster under the bed, that the neighbour is evil, that the root cellar harbours a torture chamber, that the house on the corner is haunted.

Write this story from the perspective of an adult who encounters this menace.

_____

_____

_____

_____

_____

_____

_____

_____

_____

_____

HORROR WRITING PROMPT #55

Write about this young woman in this location.

Art by Jamie Chapman. Copyright Rayne Hall.

Ideas you can use:

Who is she? Why is she here? Is she going somewhere, meeting someone, or exploring?

Does she know the area, or is she here for the first time? Perhaps she is a tourist who has lost her way at night. Maybe she was lured here with the promise of a job. What if she is here to investigate something terrible that befell her friend?

Why is she alone? What if she was here with a group of friends, but got fed up with them and struck out on her own? What if she was on a date, and the man treated her in such a shameful way that she walked away?

What is going to happen? What menace will she encounter?

Write the story from her point-of-view.

_____

_____

_____

_____

_____

_____

_____

_____

_____

_____

_____

_____

_____

_____

_____

_____

HORROR WRITING PROMPT #56

Harmless-looking animals are the planet's deadliest creatures. Why?

Ideas you can use:

What makes these animals so deadly? Do they carry diseases, or do they inject lethal poison with every sting? What if each animal takes a tiny bite out of the human body, something a person might not even notice, but they have multiplied because of recent climate change, and now they operate in swarms of millions?

Why do they appear harmless? Are they tiny insects, cuddly like cats, cute like rabbits?

Are they a new species? If yes, where do they come from - escaped from a breeding programme, released by an evil scientist, arrived with an alien spacecraft, discovered in the tropical rainforest, revived from extinction?

How many are there - just one, a dozen, or millions?

What is their habitat? Do they live in wall cracks, cow sheds, garden ponds? What do they eat?

Is the danger immediately known? Who spreads the warning about their dangers - individuals, governments, organisations? Are they believed?

What is the group with the highest risk - children, pregnant women, the elderly, or those who are HIV positive or venture into jungles?

How can humans protect themselves against these animals?

HORROR WRITING PROMPT #57

What is happening here?

Art by Chris Harvey/Dreamstime. Copyright Chris Harvey.

Ideas you can use:

Is this person dying and making one last attempt to call for help?

Is a zombie rising from its grave?

Is a giant awakening in a mountain range after thousands of years?

Who sees or hears this happening?

What does this person, zombie or giant need? What will he do to get it?

HORROR WRITING PROMPT #58

A character gains the ability to see something nobody else can see, and the sight is unbearable.

Ideas you can use:

What can she see? Other people's dark desires, evil intentions, disturbing secrets? Their opinions of her? The manner in which they will die?

What if she can see into the future? Perhaps she sees her home burning down, her community starving, her husband deserting her, a mass murderer slaughtering her children?

What if she can see when a person is lying, because their aura changes colour? Maybe she knows that a witness is giving a false statement, that her sister's fiancé lies about having no more feelings for his ex, or that a certain presidential candidate is lying about his intentions - but she can't prove it, and nobody believes her.

When and how did she acquire this ability? For dramatic purposes, it may be best if it happens suddenly, and she is slow to realise its potential.

_____

_____

_____

_____

_____

_____

_____

HORROR WRITING PROMPT #59

A collective madness grips the whole population and compels them to ritually kill all people with a certain characteristic.

Ideas you can use:

How did this collective madness take hold? Perhaps there's a virus, hypnosis, propaganda, mass hysteria, alien influence?

At first, the deaths may be attributed to something else: a serial killer, a religious cult, an extremist political group.

Who is affected? A whole town, an ethnic majority, a tribe, everyone who drinks water from a certain source?

You can write the story from the perspective of a victim, perhaps someone who has seen his parents and neighbours slaughtered and knows he is next. You could also choose the perspective of an innocent, perhaps a man suspected of being the serial killer. Another option is the point-of-view of an investigator who wants to get to the roots of this serial crime - and who may either get infected himself, or become one of the victims.

_____

_____

_____

_____

_____

_____

_____

HORROR WRITING PROMPT #60

Who is she, and why is she here?

Art by Jun-Pierre Shiozawa. Copyright Rayne Hall.

Ideas you can use:

Who is this woman? A goddess, a human, a demon, a ghost or something else?

Why is she here? Is she haunting the place where she lived, where she died, or where she committed an atrocious deed? Is she a goddess of death, appearing to tourists to foretell their impending doom? Did a curse root her to the spot, so she must remain forever while her flesh decays and the town around her falls to ruins?

What is the skeleton bird? Is it also victim of the curse, or part of the haunting? Can it fly away from the woman, or is it forever attached to her hand?

Horror Writing Prompts

HORROR WRITING PROMPT #61

An obsessive character feels wronged by someone and plots to get the justice he feels is his right.

Ideas you can use:

You can write the story from the point-of-view of the obsessed character (probably the best choice for a short story) or one of his intended victims (for a novel).

Make him a semi-sympathetic character, whom the reader can understand, but not quite like.

Who wronged him, how and why? Consider making it a genuine wrong, something that would upset, offend or enrage anyone.

Why is he not able to let go and make a new life for himself?

What reward/justice/love/vengeance does he feel entitled to? How does he go about obtaining it?

Who tries to stop him?

Does he get defeated? How, and by whom? What if he walks into the trap he laid for his intended victim? What if he sees the folly of his obsession and finally lets go - but this costs him his life or freedom?

_____

_____

_____

_____

_____

_____

_____

HORROR WRITING PROMPT #62

Write about this person.

Art by Erica Syverson. Copyright Rayne Hall.

Ideas you can use:

Is she a ghost? Some kind of spirit? An evaporating human who gradually loses substance?

Where does she live? What does she want or need?

_____

_____

_____

_____

_____

_____

_____

HORROR WRITING PROMPT #63

Many societies had a tradition of a scapegoat, where the sins and crimes of the community were formally transferred to an animal or person who was then ritually punished.

Tell the story of a human scapegoat.

Ideas you can use:

What kind of sins or crimes get transferred onto the scapegoat?

How is the scapegoat chosen? What punishment does he get? (Since you're writing horror fiction, make it slow and horrific.) Historically, the scapegoat was often driven out of the community to a certain death, for example, into the desert.

Is this a secret or official act? Is it part of the country's law, a religious observance, or a town's tradition?

Does the act need the scapegoat's consent? If yes, what might persuade him to agree? Perhaps if he refuses, they'll use his child instead. Or maybe they torture him until he is grateful for the chance of a relatively quick death. Or perhaps he is a criminal who thinks that the scapegoat penalty will actually offer him a chance to escape.

What if the scapegoat gets paid for his services? After his death, the money will support his widow and ensure the education of his children.

What if a scapegoat is chosen at random, perhaps through a lottery, or by means of an oracle?

What if a scapegoat gets chosen only in times of need (for example, during a famine) and it's based on the person's role in society at that time (for example, the youngest monk or the oldest married childless woman)?

What if a character foresees hard times and is aware that should a scapegoat be needed, it will be him? How will he try to avert the fate?

What if the wealthy person who's due to be sacrificed as the scapegoat bribes the officials so they choose someone else instead?

_____

_____

_____

_____

_____

_____

_____

_____

_____

_____

_____

_____

_____

_____

_____

_____

HORROR WRITING PROMPT #64

A building devours those who live in it.

Ideas you can use:

What kind of building is it: a skyscraper? A villa? A holiday cottage? A castle? A terraced house in London's East End?

Why does the building devour its inhabitants? Perhaps the builders neglected a certain ritual, such as the burying of a slaughtered cockerel under the threshold, and now the building is forever hungry.

How long do people live in the building before they become prey?

Is everyone affected, or only certain types of people - perhaps only women, or only adults, or only those who sleep in the eastern tower?

How does the building devour them - physically or metaphorically? Do people fall sick and die, or do they gradually merge into the walls?

_____

_____

_____

_____

_____

_____

_____

_____

_____

HORROR WRITING PROMPT #65

Write about this picture.

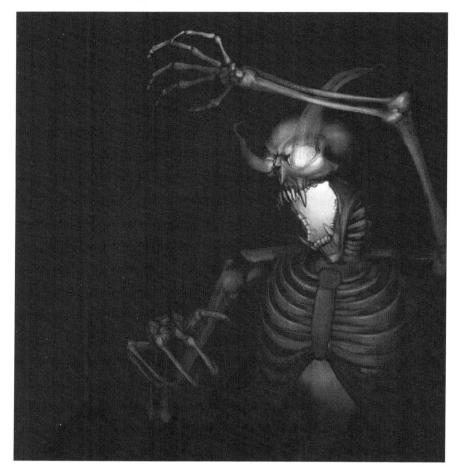

Art by Stephanie Mendoza. Copyright Rayne Hall.

Ideas you can use:

Is this skeleton a sentient creature? Is it a dead skeleton, but inhabited by a spirit?

Where do the light and the smoke come from?

Horror Writing Prompts

HORROR WRITING PROMPT #66

Write about an unusual execution method.

Ideas you can use:

Start by inventing the method. Since you're writing horror, make it slow and gruesome.

If you like you can research execution methods online. Some of them are so cruel it's hard to believe that humans are capable of this. Vary them with your own vivid imagination. You may also want to involve psychological cruelty.

What crime gets punished by this method? This is probably a crime particularly abhorred by that society. However, it can also be a punishment meted out by a tyrant to all who resist him - people who refuse to surrender their town when he besieges them or women who refuse to have sex with him.

Are the executions public, as a deterrent to others?

_____

_____

_____

_____

_____

_____

_____

_____

_____

HORROR WRITING PROMPT #67

Write a story from the perspective of someone who sees this person and feels both fear and compassion.

Art by José Manuel Ayala Sandoval. Copyright Rayne Hall.

Ideas you can use:

What is this - a zombie? Something else? Why are parts of the face intact and others missing? Why are the teeth pointed - did they grow this way, or were they filed to points?

How did he come to be like this?

What does he want or need now?

Horror Writing Prompts

HORROR WRITING PROMPT #68

A person schemes to trap another, priding himself in his ingenuity, and falls into his own trap.

Ideas you can use:

Who seeks to trap whom? Why and how?

For a novel, you can use the point of view of the perpetrator, the victim or a witness.

For a short story, consider the perspective of the would-be perpetrator. He realises too late that the opponent has laid a trap for her. With his scheming, he has walked straight into the trap.

_____

_____

_____

_____

_____

_____

_____

_____

_____

_____

_____

_____

_____

HORROR WRITING PROMPT #69

Whom does this demon beckon? To where or what?

Art by Jamie Chapman. Copyright Rayne Hall.

Horror Writing Prompts

Ideas you can use:

Demons are intelligent and manipulative. They often have a seductive quality, and they use a human's own desires to make him do what they want.

First think about a victim, someone the demon manipulates. Then select what the demon wants this person to do.

Why does the person fall for the demon's seduction?

_____

_____

_____

_____

_____

_____

_____

_____

_____

_____

_____

_____

_____

_____

_____

_____

HORROR WRITING PROMPT #70

A gardener (or animal breeder) finally succeeds in growing a new plant (or animal), but the new life form develops into something he cannot control.

Ideas you can use:

If possible, write about something you're familiar with. If you're an amateur gardener, write about plants, and if you're a dog lover, focus on canines. This will give your story authenticity and plausibility.

Does the gardener or breeder know he's taking a risk? Does someone try to dissuade him? Is he breaking laws to achieve the breakthrough?

In what ways is the new plant or animal dangerous? When does he realise it?

What steps does he do to capture or destroy his creation?

_____

_____

_____

_____

_____

_____

_____

_____

_____

_____

HORROR WRITING PROMPT #71

During a pleasant stroll, a walker makes a gruesome discovery.

Ideas you can use:

What does she find? An amputated hand? A gigantic tentacle that definitely doesn't belong to a native species?

Emphasise the gruesome or macabre nature of the find by contrasting it with the innocuous, pleasant surroundings. Perhaps the severed hand lies in a flowerbed in the public park, surrounded by cheerfully nodding daffodils. Maybe the giant tentacle lies on the golden beach where only a few hours before children built sandcastles.

Consider the character who makes the discovery, and how her personal situation may complicate matters.

What if she's a tourist and doesn't speak enough of the local language to explain to the police what she has seen?

What if she's disabled and can't get close enough to the find to be sure of its nature? Maybe she uses her crutch to turn the thing over, and discovers that it is worse than she thought.

What if she's an illegal immigrant, or on the run from the law, and can't risk reporting her discovery to the police?

What if she's drunk alcohol or smoked weed and still smells of it, so nobody takes her bizarre talk seriously?

What if the thing she finds has a personal meaning for her, something she recognises and understands even if nobody else does?

Horror Writing Prompts

HORROR WRITING PROMPT #72

Pets turn against their owners.

Ideas you can use:

What kind of pets? Dogs, cats, hamsters, cornsnakes? If possible, write about animals of which you have personal experience. This means you won't need to spend much time on research, and your story will feel authentic and plausible.

Why do pets turn against their owners? Are they staging a revolution to subdue the human race and rule the world? Are they taking revenge for abuse? Are they fighting to gain their freedom? What if a virus infection has turned all animals of a species mad?

Do all pets turn against their owners? Only those of a certain species? Only those with a grudge to avenge?

How do the humans protect themselves?

_____

_____

_____

_____

_____

_____

_____

_____

_____

_____

HORROR WRITING PROMPT #73

A character has an organ removed against his will. It will be transplanted into someone else's body.

Ideas you can use:

What organ gets removed? Can he survive without it, or will he die? (For example, does he have one kidney removed or both?)

Who are the harvesters? Doctors at the local hospital? Holiday reps at a tourist camp? An ailing mafia boss's minions?

How did the harvesters get the character into their power? Was he abducted, together with many other victims? Or was he kidnapped for ransom, and when his family didn't pay up, his abductors decided to make money from him in another way?

Is he the only victim, or is there a big international harvest trading ring? What if the organ harvesters pick vulnerable victims who won't be missed or whose disappearance won't be reported to the authorities - homeless people, refugees, illegal immigrants?

How hygienic and safe is the procedure? Is it carried out by highly qualified doctors or by quacks in primitive surroundings?

Who are the recipients? Rich people in wealthy nations? Important people such as rulers, royals and spiritual leaders? Do the recipients know that the donors did not give their organs willingly?

_____

_____

_____

_____

_____

HORROR WRITING PROMPT #74

Whom does this beast menace?

Art by Michelle Greaves. Copyright Rayne Hall.

Ideas you can use:

What is this animal? A kind of dog? Something else? Is it a living creature or some kind of spirit?

Where does it live?

What does it feed on (other than human flesh)? When and where does it hunt?

What does it need?

HORROR WRITING PROMPT #75

A building project requires a human sacrifice at its foundations.

Ideas you can use:

Sacrifices - often animal, sometimes human - were common in several prehistoric and historic societies. The victim was killed and buried either under the hearth or under the threshold. You may want to research what is known about these customs, or invent your own.

What is the underlying belief? Does the human sacrifice serve to appease the gods or to protect the building?

Does every new building need a human sacrifice, or only public buildings, monuments and royal residences?

How does the sacrificial human get selected - is it someone perceived to be of low value in this society and therefore dispensable (a convicted criminal, a cripple, an elderly person about to die anyway), or someone considered to be of high value and therefore a fitting gift to the gods (a princess, or a particularly beautiful girl, a healthy child, a skilled craftswoman, an accomplished warrior)? Perhaps tradition demands a specific person, such as the architect's eldest daughter, or the first stranger who enters the town on that day.

What is the killing method? What is the ritual? You may want to research human sacrifice traditions.

What happens if the intended victim escapes? Will the builders kill a substitute?

What if an important building gets erected without the sacrifice, and the gods punish the community for this neglect?

HORROR WRITING PROMPT #76

A character believes that a supposedly dangerous object/ creature/person is harmless, and sets out to tame and use it.

Ideas you can use:

What is this person, object, animal or creature?

Why is it believed to be dangerous, evil or harmful?

Why does the character believe otherwise?

How does she set out about befriending/taming/saving the creature? She may devote all her time and resources to this. Make it difficult for her, with many setbacks as well as encouraging results.

Who opposes her attempts? Colleagues? Family? Experts? The government?

Perhaps she achieves success at last. While enjoying her triumph, she lets her guard down, and discovers too late that the animal/ person/creature/object is dangerous/evil after all.

A short story may end with this discovery, implying her impending doom. A novel may continue for longer, showing the creature gaining power, and its former owner the only one who knows enough about its habits to have a chance at defeating it.

_____

_____

_____

_____

_____

_____

HORROR WRITING PROMPT #77

What happens in this abandoned building?

Photo: Creative Commons Stock Photos. (Photographer not specified.)

Ideas you can use:

What was this building's purpose before it closed down? What sinister actions took place here? What remnants of those activities remain?

Who uses this site now, and for what? What secret or illegal activities take place now? What if a gang uses the building to keep prisoners or to carry out interrogations under torture or to execute traitors?

Who wrote the graffiti, and who placed the chair in the light?

SAMPLE STORY: FOUR BONY HANDS

To show how you can weave fiction around the prompts, here is a short story I wrote based on Horror Writing Prompt #35 - Tell a fairy tale from the perspective of the villain.

FOUR BONY HANDS

by Rayne Hall

It was February, the time of Imbolc, and frost painted ice flowers on the window panes.

In the cosy warmth of her cottage in the clearing, Estelle munched freshly baked gingerbread and sipped hot cinnamon tea. She was spreading her tarot cards – The Knight of Wands: an unexpected visitor; the Five of Chalices: unseen danger – when she became aware of movements outside.

Sparrows and blacktits fluttered up from the windowsill. A moment later, a wee fist scooped the oatflakes Estelle had sprinkled there.

She jumped up and dashed out of the door. She caught the offender, a boy of five or six who trembled in her grip.

"What do you think, stealing the food from the hungry birds?" she scolded.

The laddie just stared, wide-eyed. He wore neither hat nor gloves, and his fingers and nose were purple.

Intuitively, Estelle knew. "You've run away from home, haven't you?"

A dirty girl crawled from under the bushes. "We're not going back, never - ever - ever!" she shouted. "And if you try to make us, I'll bite you!"

"How many days have you been alone in the forest? You're fair jeelit! Come inside and get some warmth and food. Do you like gingerbread?"

Once inside, the children clutched their hands around steaming earthenware mugs. They gobbled up apples, wholemeal bannock and gingerbread with a desperation that made Estelle wonder if they'd ever been fed properly at home. Both had the black-tinged aura of people traumatised by abuse.

"I'm Estelle. What are your names?" When she received no reply, she took the boy's icy hand. "Crivvens! You're so thin! Your fingers are only skin and bone."

He pulled his hand away and hid it behind his back.

Astarte, the black cat, hissed. She didn't like strangers.

For a long time, the boy stared at the steamed-up window, as if hypnotised by the stained-glass picture hanging there. "That's the devil."

"It's good to hear you have a voice to speak after all." Estelle smiled. "That isn't the devil. He's the Horned God of the forest. He's wearing deer antlers. But I'll hide the picture if you don't like it." She stood up and drew the tea-dyed crochet curtains across the window.

"He's the devil," the boy insisted, staring at her with intense, blue, madness-glazed eyes. "And you're a witch."

She gave him her standard reply: "If by 'witch' you mean 'Wise Woman with her Wits About Her', I'll wear that pointed hat gladly," but he didn't seem to understand.

"I've seen witches on DVD." He pointed his scrawny finger at the large pentagram dangling on Estelle's chest. "They all have these things, that's why I know."

Estelle sighed. There was no point in explaining Wiccan beliefs to the boy. For him, a witch was an evil magical creature who lived in a forest, together with vampires, werewolves and whatnots.

"Watching DVDs is not good for you," she said. She had opted out of media consumerism long ago. "Have another piece of bannock."

"You just want to fatten me up."

"Well, you need fattening up, don't you think? You're as thin as a little sparrow."

Without warning, he kicked the cat. Astarte miaowed, hissed, curled her back and glared at the boy with hatred.

"You shouldn't do that," Estelle reprimanded him. "Astarte hasn't done anything to you."

"She's a witch's cat," he said, as if that justified everything. And for good measure, he kicked her again, this time so hard that her body hurled across the stone-flagged floor. She howled and coiled into ball of raised fur under the oven bench.

"That's enough!" Estelle slammed a palm on the table. "You're guests in my home, and while you're here, you behave. And if you don't, I'll take you right back to your parents. Just see if I don't!"

That silenced them.

Compassion and unease tugged at Estelle's heart, pulled it in opposing directions. She sensed an aura of aggression clinging to them like a bad smell. But this was hardly their fault. They were wee bairns, victims of abuse by family, society and media influence. Her pulse accelerated, thudding in her chest and throat. She took belly breaths to calm her fears and focused her attention on lighting beeswax candles. The honey fragrance nearly succeeded in calming her.

All three sat in silence. Estelle waited for the water in big copper kettle to simmer. The lassie held her hands squeezed between her thighs and refused to meet Estelle's eyes, while the boy's blue pupils seethed with cold fire.

When the water had heated at last, Estelle filled the old-fashioned tin bath, adding splashes of eucalyptus and ginger oil. She put both children in the tub together. Their bodies were so thin their ribs showed, and their thighs were flecked with purple bruises.

When Estelle saw the angry welts on the boy's buttocks, pity overwhelmed her and drove the dislike from her soul. "Losh!" She softened her voice. "Did your father do that?"

"With his belt," the girl said. "And if you make us go back, I'll kill you." Her voice was hard.

Horror Writing Prompts

"I won't. You'll stay with me for tonight, and tomorrow I'll take you to…"

"We don't want to stay. You can't make us."

"Oh yes, I can," Estelle said, and pushed the door bolts in place. The upper one was out of the children's reach and would ensure they could not sneak out at night. "It's for your own good. Another night in the snell wind, and you'd freeze to death."

"Witch!" the boy yelled.

"Come here." Estelle tried to rub them with the oven-warmed towel. The girl fled the contact, and the boy kicked out, so she left them to dry themselves.

"Time to sleep," she said. "The bed is much nicer than the forest floor, you'll see."

She owned a single bed. Her cottage was not equipped for visitors. She decided that the children needed the comfort of the bed more than she did. Perhaps she would spend the night awake, or else she could try to ease into sleep while curling in the rocking chair. Tiredness gnawed at her brain.

She shook the crumbles of dried basil and lavender from her spare linen and changed the sheets. She ushered the kids into the bed and tucked them in. They lay side by side, stiff and brittle like sticks. Their hostility filled the cottage like a bad odour.

She spoke a Wiccan blessing over them. "Sleep well."

They did not reply.

As soon as she turned away, they started to whisper. They kept whispering a long time, but always ceased as soon as she looked at them.

Estelle had intended to let the fire die down, sweep the embers aside and use the oven to bake another batch of rye loaves overnight. But the children, after Brigid knew how many days and nights in the Highland cold, would need all the warmth they could get. She would keep the heat going for them, building it to a cosy glaise. She opened the cast iron grate and fed more logs into the hungry flames.

She would not be able to sleep in the overheated cottage, with or without bed. She wrapped herself in her crochet blanket as a protection – against what, she could not say. It was only for a single night.

She pitied the children, but could not like them. Perhaps, growing up in an environment of abuse and violence, they simply had not had a chance to learn about love and kindness. What they needed was sympathetic but firm guidance. A foster family, perhaps. She would let them sleep in her home for a night, and then – what?

She shoved a large chunk of a storm-felled tree into the oven's domed mouth. Then she spread the tarot, entreating the cards to tell her what to do.

First came the Emperor, symbol of authority, and it frightened her. The law was still after her because she had damaged military property, sprayed graffiti on a corrupt politician's house, and hijacked a truck of sheep destined for the slaughterhouse. As long as she stayed hidden in this dilapidated forest cottage, she was safe. If she took the children into town and handed them over to the authorities, someone would ask for her ID, and she would lose her freedom.

She knew what the next cards would be even before she turned them. The Wheel of Fortune, reversed. And finally, Death, signifying an ending or loss.

The cat glanced up sympathetically.

"I'll do what's right." Estelle decided at last. "Even if I lose everything. I can't let innocent bairns suffer."

She fed the oven with resin-rich logs. The heat would melt the children's fears, and her own. The cat, sprawled on the bench by the oven, basked in the glowing warmth.

Just when the fire was really hot, the children slid out of bed and sneaked up to Estelle. Only Astarte's sudden hiss alerted her.

"What's the -"

Four bony hands clawed into Estelle's flesh.

"Witch, witch!" the children cried. "Wicked witch!"

They pushed her towards the gaping door of the big, hungry oven.

DEAR READER,

My dream is that one day I'll read a great horror novel, and in the Acknowledgements section it says "Thanks also to Rayne Hall, whose prompt inspired me to write this book."

I hope you will weave some scary stories around these ideas, and that they will propel your fiction on the path to success. Above all, I hope that you have had fun playing with these prompts.

I'd love it if you could post a review on Amazon or some other book site where you have an account and posting privileges. Maybe you can mention what kind of fiction you write, and which of the prompts you found most inspiring.

Email me the link to your review, and I'll send you a free review copy (ebook) of one of my other Writer's Craft books. Let me know which one you would like: *Writing Fight Scenes, Writing Scary Scenes, The Word-Loss Diet, Writing About Magic, Writing About Villains, Writing Dark Stories, Euphonics For Writers, Writing Short Stories to Promote Your Novels, Twitter for Writers, Why Does My Book Not Sell? 20 Simple Fixes, Writing Vivid Settings, How To Train Your Cat To Promote Your Book, Writing Deep Point of View, Getting Book Reviews, Novel Revision Prompts, Writing Vivid Dialogue, Writing Vivid Characters, Writing Book Blurbs and Synopses, Writing Vivid Plots, Write Your Way Out Of Depression: Practical Self-Therapy For Creative Writers, Mid-Novel Revision Prompts, Fantasy Writing Prompts.*

My email is contact@raynehall.com. Also, drop me a line if you've spotted any typos which have escaped the proof-reader's eagle eyes, or want to give me private feedback or have questions.

You can also contact me on Twitter: https://twitter.com/RayneHall. Tweet me that you've read this book, and I'll probably follow you back.

If you find this book helpful, it would be great if you could spread the word about it. Maybe you know other writers who would benefit.

I'm also adding an excerpt from another Writer's Craft guide you may find useful: *Writing Scary Scenes*. I hope you like it.

With best wishes for your creativity and inspiration,

Rayne Hall

ACKNOWLEDGEMENTS

I give sincere thanks to the beta readers and critiquers who read the draft chapters and offered valuable feedback: Larisa Walk, Douglas Kolacki, Phillip T. Stephens, Leigh Grissom, Dr JA d'Merricksson, Les Burns and everyone else who chimed in with feedback and suggestions.

The book cover is by Erica Syverson and Uros Jovanovic. Jonathan Broughton proof-read the manuscript, and Bogdan Matei formatted the book.

And finally, I say thank you to my sweet black cat Sulu who snuggled on the desk between my arms with his paw on my wrist and purred his approval as I typed, especially when I mentioned animals.

Rayne Hall

EXCERPT FROM WRITING SCARY SCENES

Here are two sample chapters from another Writer's Craft book, *Writing Scary Scenes*, which you may find useful.

CHAPTER 5: SOUNDS BUILD SUSPENSE

Of all the senses, the sense of hearing serves best to create excitement, suspense and fear, so use it liberally.

Mention and describe several sounds, and insert those sentences in different sections of the scene. This technique suits all stories in all genres. It works especially well if the scene is set in darkness, because the sense of hearing is sharpened when the vision is reduced.

ACTION SOUNDS

Use the sounds of the ongoing action, especially of the threat: the villain's footsteps clanking down the metal stairs, the dungeon door squealing open, the rasp of the prison guard's voice, the attack dog's growl, the rattling of the torture instruments in the tool box.

BACKGROUND SOUNDS

In addition, use the background noises which aren't connected to the action. Think about the noises of the setting.

Examples

A shutter banged against the frame.

A car door slammed. A motor whined.

Horror Writing Prompts

A dog howled in the distance.

The motor stuttered and whined.

The ceiling fan whirred.

The wind whined.

The rope clanked rhythmically against the flagpole.

Computers beeped, phones shrilled, and printers whirred.

Waves hissed against the shore.

Waves thumped against the hull.

Thunder rumbled.

Rodent feet scurried.

Water gurgled in the drainpipe.

EXTREME SUSPENSE

A few 'sound' sentences work wonders for the atmosphere of your scary scene. You can insert them wherever it makes sense - and even in random places.

The most powerful use of this technique is to make a suspenseful moment even more suspenseful.

By inserting a sentence about an irrelevant background noise, you can slow the pace without lowering the excitement. This turns the tension and suspense up several notches.

Here's an example:

Before

The knife came closer to her throat. And closer.

She squirmed against the bonds, knowing it to be useless.

The cold edge of steel touched her skin. She tried not to swallow.

After

The knife came closer to her throat. And closer.

She squirmed against the bonds, knowing it to be useless.

Somewhere in the distance, a car door slammed and a motor whined.

The cold edge of steel touched her skin. She tried not to swallow.

COLLECTING SOUNDS

Whenever you're away from home and have a few moments to spare, listen to the noises around you. Jot them down in your writer's notebook. (If you don't have a writer's notebook yet, get one: a small lightweight one with ruled pages is practical.)

If possible, describe what the noises sound like, using verbs (*a car rattles up the road* or *a car whines up the road*)

By observing and noting the noises of one place per day (365 places per year), you can build a fantastic resource which will come in handy for future fiction projects. This is also a handy way of killing time, especially in boring meetings, at the laundrette, at the railway station, in a queue, and in the dentist's waiting room. Use the time constructively for writing research.

You can even swap noise notes with other writers. Your writing buddy may be working on a scene set in an abandoned mine-shaft - and you may have notes about the sounds in such a place. Or you may write a scene set in the Brazilian jungle - where she took notes during her trip last year.

CHAPTER 6: TOTAL ISOLATION

Solitary adventures are more dangerous than group adventures. In nature, an animal which becomes separated from the herd is vulnerable to predators. To make your scene scary, let your heroine face the danger alone.

The more you isolate your protagonist, the more frightening the scene becomes. Think of as many ways as possible to make her even more cut off from rescue and moral support.

SEND THE ALLIES AWAY

Give your protagonist a reason why she faces this danger on her own.

Perhaps she has no choice: the little girl is alone in the house because her parents have gone to the theatre. The hero's guide and friends have been killed leaving him as the only survivor. The explorer's companions have stolen his equipment and deserted him. The prisoner escaped from the dungeon and is fleeing alone.

On the other hand, she may have chosen to do this alone: the treasure hunter doesn't want to share the bounty with others. The teenager quarrelled with her date and told him to leave her alone. The explorer is the only one who believes that the coded map reveals the true location of the temple; when others mocked his belief, he set out on his own.

Sometimes, when the adventure stretches over several scenes, you can take away the protagonist's companions one by one. First, his friends declare him crazy and refuse to join the expedition, so he sets out with his girlfriend, three mates, and a local guide. Then his girlfriend falls in love with one of his mates, and the two depart. The local guide steals the equipment and deserts. One of his loyal companions gets killed by a giant snake, the second by the evil overlord's poisoned arrow. Now he's alone.

In other works of fiction, the protagonist may be alone for only part of the scene. For example, the hero and heroine are exploring the castle ruins together. Then the hero gets captured by the villains, or maybe he leaves the group to fetch supplies from the car or to investigate a mysterious signal, and the heroine faces the danger alone. For the last part of the scene, they're together again, but the danger is not yet over.

CUT THE LINES OF COMMUNICATION

To isolate your protagonist even more, deprive her of the means of calling for help. The villains have cut the telephone lines. A blizzard prevents other people from coming to this place. The radio battery is empty so the explorer can no longer send Morse signals. The computer has crashed. The internet server is down.

For the writer of scary scenes, mobile phones (American: "cell phones") are a nuisance. The scene isn't really scary if your heroine can summon help at any time. Make sure she doesn't have a mobile phone with her, or that it isn't functioning: Her bag was stolen, or she lost it during her daring escape or had to drop it while running for her life. She doesn't own a mobile phone because she hates modern technology. There is no reception in the remote mountain valley. She forgot to recharge the battery. She couldn't afford to pay for a top-up. She borrowed a friend's mobile phone and the friend forgot to tell her that the service has been disconnected.

NOBODY KNOWS

There must be no chance of a lucky rescue, either. Nobody must miss her, or even know where she is. The treasure hunter laid a false trail about his destination. The teenager didn't tell her parents where she was going because she knew they wouldn't approve. The police officer did not tell her colleagues because what she plans on doing is not strictly legal. The heroine tells no one where she's going because she doesn't want her stalking ex-boyfriend to find her. The hiker told the landlord of the last inn that he planned to walk south, but then changed his mind and went west.

PROFESSIONAL EXAMPLES

Copyright rules prevent me from quoting excerpts longer than a few lines, so I can't show you examples of how professional writers use this technique. However, you'll find that many bestselling authors use it in their fiction. Among Victorian writers, Amelia Edwards excelled at it. Among modern horror writers, Stephen King has used this technique in many of his stories.

DRAWBACKS

This technique does not work for every story. Some plots require that two or more people face the danger together. You may be able to compromise, for example, the heroine and hero stay together, but they lose their mobile phone and are unable to summon help.

Made in the USA
San Bernardino, CA
22 July 2017